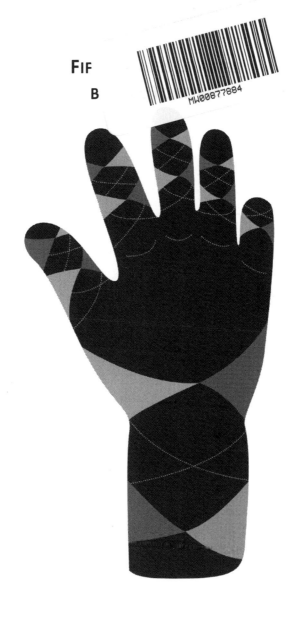

Like Phil on Facebook: Facebook.com/SuchaNiceGuy
Follow Phil on Twitter: @PhilTorcivia
Blog: PhilTorcivia.blogspot.com
Author website: Torcivia.com

*Nothing in this book is true except my desire to cover my ass
with this statement.*

Cover designed by Anna V. Chastain of ChastainGraphics.com
Copy editing by Marguerite Walker II and Jessica Dearborn
Author photo by Micaela Malmi of EpicPhotoJournalism.com
ISBN: 147758353X
ISBN-13: 978-1477583531

CHAPTER ONE

Marriage is not living with the person you love,
but living with the person you can't live without.
— Aissa Amor A. Sarmiento

She said yes. Now what? Can this work long term, or is it all a game to Bea? In my fifty-plus years, I've never been exposed to such kinkiness. I must admit, it's not bad. Still, I worry about keeping up with my little minx. Mormon Silver may need help with this one.

After she accepts my proposal (*thank goodness*), we watch the game while kind fans offer congratulations. I prefer tequila to calm my nerves, but am gracious. Bea beams as she stares at the ring. I beam as I stare at her.

"Sweetie, I wish I could afford something more substantial."

"Don't be silly. The fact that this was handed down through generations makes it priceless," Bea assures me, as she squeezes my thigh and kisses my cheek. "We're going to the Hyatt after the game and I'm going to give you a proper thank you."

"If you insist."

The Padres lose, as usual. Bea was cool about staying until the final out. It drives me crazy when fans abandon their team. Anything can happen in baseball, regardless of the score, until that final out.

Outside the stadium, Bea insists we take a rickshaw to the Hyatt. *Great. I get to smell the Eastern European man-stank of the driver for eight blocks.* As we cruise along, Bea keeps grabbing my package, teasing me.

"Quit it. I don't want to be walking into the Hyatt with wood," I whisper.

"Really? Ooh, you *are* becoming engorged."

"Engorged? I'm certainly at half-mast."

"I love it, Sailor Mormon."

I tip the rickshaw driver. *Let's hope he spends it on deodorant.* We walk through the lobby to the elevator, and I see that familiar look in Bea's face: Something kinky will be going down while we're going up. We step into the elevator (*thank God, alone*) and head to the 43rd floor. No chance we're making it all the way. *Fuck. There had better not be cameras in here.*

Bea pulls out the stop button around the twentieth floor, and all hell breaks loose. She slams me up against the wall and undoes my jeans in record time. Her mouth is so warm and wet around me as she looks up occasionally to see how close I am to exploding. *So damn close. Think of something non-sexual, Mormon, quick!*

I used to be able to think about sports like hockey and baseball to delay my ejaculation, but Bea has ruined those counter-fantasies. All I can think of is recipes. I begin mentally concocting the design of my own natural protein bar.

Bea tugs at my testicles every time she senses I'm close. *She's quite skilled.* I close my eyes and concentrate.

"You're not coming yet, mister. You can peek over the edge, but tonight we're going over together."

"Two cups of natural peanut butter ..."

"What?"

"Oh, sorry."

The elevator alarm starts to ring. I panic and push in the button to stop the ringing. Bea laughs and stands up as I quickly yank up my jeans. Naturally, Mormon-luck kicks in and the elevator stops at the next floor. The doors open to an elderly woman. My purple torpedo pokes through the zipper of my jeans and points directly toward the poor woman, who stands with her mouth agape.

"Oh, hey, Grandma. This is my fiancé, Mormon Silver."

Down boy.

CHAPTER TWO

I only drink to make other people seem interesting.
– George Jean Nathan

I turn away, zip up, and extend a hand to greet Grandma. "Hi. It's a pleasure to meet you."

"I can see that," she responds with a look of disgust, ignoring my extended hand.

"Oh, yes, sorry about that. I have a condition."

"Come upstairs for a nightcap, Grandma," Bea insists.

"You have Christian Brothers?"

"I do."

"Fine," Grandma agrees as she enters the elevator and stands in the opposite corner, studying me. "I thought you were done with older men. Where did you find this one?"

"Oh, he's darling. Wait till you get to know him."

"I'm not *that* much older."

"... if you're counting in dog years," Grandma sneers.

"So, how about those Padres?" Bea asks, trying to change the subject.

Finally, the elevator dings and the doors open to the 43rd floor.

"After you, my dear," I charm.

"I know better than to walk in front of an armed man. Scoot!"

This old sack is going to be hard to crack.

I sheepishly lead the way. Once in Bea's condo, I head straight to the bar.

"I'm going to freshen up. You two get acquainted," Bea suggests as she abandons me.

"How do you take your brandy, Ma'am?"

"Like my men: neat."

"I'm glad you didn't say 'stiff.'"

"Excuse me?"

"I said, did you have a nice trip?"

"Trip where?"

"Here. I assume you're visiting from out of town?"

"I own this building."

"Oh." *Shitboogers.*

I pour her brandy, along with three fingers of Maker's Mark to sedate me. I hand one glass to her. She continues to scowl.

"What exactly do you do, Mr. Silver?"

"Let's have some fun. Guess."

"Plumber?"

Hag.

"Nope."

"Shopping cart collector?"

I so want to drop the C-word.

"Nope."

"Paperboy?"

Is it legal to kick an old woman in the baby hole?

"Nope, but you're close. Give up?"

"I do."

"I'm a blogger."

"A what?"

"Blogger. A writer who writes things for the web."

"Does one make a good living as a blobber?"

"*Blogger.* Good enough."

She gets up into my space. She's less than five feet tall, yet I'm intimidated.

"For some people, but certainly not good enough for my granddaughter," she insists as she tweaks my nipple. I squeak like a schoolgirl on the playground.

CHAPTER THREE

If it is true that we have sprung from the ape, there are occasions when my own spring appears not to have been very far. – Cornelia Otis Skinner

Worried that I might belt the woman, and confident she could kick my ass, I excuse myself, and join Bea in the master suite.

"So, how are you two getting along?"

"About as well as Kardashians and skinny jeans. Can I throw spoons at her, or at least give her a noogie? Please?"

"Now, darling, it's important you win her over."

"Not possible."

"Find a way."

"Seriously?"

"Yes. Grandma is my only hope of emerging from these financial difficulties. She holds the key to the safe, so to speak, and she's here auditing my businesses to get our affairs back in order."

"Can I at least drug her?"

"No! You go out there and make nice. I'll be out in a few minutes."

I put on my fake smile and return to the family room. Grandma is futzing with the TV remote.

"Why won't this work? Things were much easier in my day; you pulled the button and turned the knob. Two through thirteen, UHF, and VHF."

"Here, let me try," I insist as she pulls the remote away from my reach.

"I'm not helpless. If you want to make yourself useful, refill my beverage, blobber."

"*Blogger.* Another arsenic rocks?"

"What did you say?"

"Another up or on the rocks?"

"Neat, you nitwit."

As I pour the biddy her drink, I see the TV picture coming into focus.

"There. Finally. Oh, dear Lord!"

"Now what? Isn't *Green Acres* on?"

"Buh ... wha ... is that ...?"

I step back from the wet bar to get a gander. I see a sixty-inch high definition picture of myself bound to the bed, wearing Canadiens panties. *Fuck! It's the video from that crazy night.* I run to the front of the TV and begin pushing buttons. Finally, the power is off. Bea emerges from the bedroom just in time to see me fifty shades of red.

"You ought to be ashamed of yourself."

"I know, right? Ordinarily, I wouldn't be caught dead wearing blue and red."

"What's going on?" Bea asks.

"That man is a big pervert who wears women's undergarments."

"I'm not *that* big. I've been cutting back on carbs, actually," I insist while patting my belly.

Grandma storms out in a huff. *Fine by me.* Bea giggles.

"Why is that on your TV, you naughty Lovergirl?"

"I think Eric was watching it ... while masturbating."

"Christ."

"Kidding. I was watching it. I know you're not crazy about the ending, but the part leading up to it was smokin' hot, if you ask me."

"Lovely."

"Listen, you need to promise me you'll use your charm on Grandma. We need her support."

"Ugh."

"If you do this for me, Uncle M, I'll do *this* for you," she says as she grabs my package.

"We have unfinished business from the elevator, don't we? My turn." I lift and set her on the loveseat. I remove her sweatpants. *She's pantyless. How convenient and delicious!* "Oh, look: Grandma left her brandy. Can't let that go to waste."

I take the crystal tumbler and drizzle brandy into her bellybutton. I lick gently as the brandy river winds its way toward her spot. The coolness of the alcohol teases, as her clit dances around my tongue. I'm drunk on the sweet combination with Lovergirl's juices. As Bea arches into climax, the front door swings open.

"I left in such a hurry I forgot my ... oh, for the love of ... you're disgusting—the both of you."

I slump down and rest my cheek against Bea's abdomen as Grandma grabs her purse, leaves, and slams the door. Bea runs her fingers through my hair as we giggle.

This won't be easy.

13

CHAPTER FOUR

Write the bad things that are done to you in sand, but write the good things that happen to you on a piece of marble. – Anonymous

After a night of proper, horizontal celebration about our engagement, I decide to sneak out of bed and make a nice breakfast for my princess. Cooking is a passion, and a great way for me to decompress. I slide on my boxer-briefs, and stumble foggy-eyed into the kitchen. I open the fridge, grab eggs, and begin searching beneath the stove for a pan. Suddenly, I hear a spoon clinking against the side of a glass. *Where am I, at a wedding reception?*

I turn to find Grandma seated at the breakfast nook wearing reading glasses while browsing the Union Tribune.

"Be a good boy and warm up my coffee," she orders as she slides the mug in my direction.

"Huh?"

"Oh, and put on a shirt, will you? I wouldn't want to find one of your silver chest hairs in my eggs."

"Grandma, what are you doing here?"

"You may call me by my proper name, Silver."

"Which is?"

"Gertrude Aspinwald ... Ms. A, if you like."

Silly name.

"Fine," I agree as I carry the pot of coffee over and top off her mug. She doesn't look up.

I retreat to the bedroom, grab my shirt off the floor, and return—no longer a health risk.

"So, Ms. A, how would you like your eggs?"

"Two whites with one yolk over easy. Fry up some bacon too. I prefer it crisp, but not burned."

"Don't you have room service here?"

She's testing me...

"Of course. Don't you know how to separate eggs?"

... and I'm not giving in.

"Of course."

"Then you best get a-crackin'. You have a long day ahead of you."

"In fact, I do. I've fallen behind in my blogging. I was supposed to interview Bea, and in two blinks I'm halfway down the aisle."

"Not even one-tenth the way."

I ignore her sass and begin cooking silently. I can feel her eyes. The TV remote is sitting on the counter, so I flip on the TV to catch some news. Naturally, in my groggy, yet agitated state I forget the video of yours truly strapped to the bed is still loaded. Grandma snickers. I hit the "Source" button and finally find the news.

"You know something, maybe you should interview me for your blob."

"Blog. B-L-O-G."

"Whatever."

"What, of interest, would you have for my readers?"

"Plenty. We could talk about my empire, how my father became rich by investing in Canadian oil fields, how I'm going to turn this property back into the thriving Mecca it once was."

"Hm."

"Or, I could tell you all about my granddaughter Bea's *other* fiancé."

"WHAT?"

I'm wide-awake now.

CHAPTER FIVE

It is not a lack of love, but a lack of friendship that makes unhappy marriages. – Friedrich Nietzsche

"I never said yes," Bea says as she enters the kitchen.

"An insignificant technicality," the beast insists.

"Wait a minute," I interrupt, "you're already engaged to someone else?"

"No. Not really."

"Yes, she is," insists Grandma, "I witnessed the proposal. Sorry, blubber, you're too late."

"BLOGGER."

"How are those eggs coming along? Don't let them get dry."

The nerve of this woman!

I remove the pan from the fire and try to process what I'm hearing.

"Bea? Are you engaged to someone else or not?"

"No, of course not. He asked, but I wasn't interested."

"Who is he?"

"That's not important."

"Chris," Grandma volunteers, "and he's young, successful, and quite dashing."

Bea walks over and wraps her arms around me from behind.

"You know I love you. He's just an insignificant detail from my past."

"Show him the ring," Grandma suggests.

What a relentless woman.

"Wait, there's a ring? I thought you didn't accept."

"It's in my dresser somewhere. He refused to take it back. This is the only ring with meaning," Bea says while showing us the one I gave her. *That's my girl.*

"Well, I'll let you two work out the terms of your parting ways. I have work to do. You can come back and interview me at noon, blobber."

I sigh and count to five.

"What about your eggs, Ms. A?"

"I've changed my mind. Think I'll have a scone."

She gathers her newspaper and purse, and leaves wearing a smirk.

I'm not sure what's going on. There are dozens of questions floating around my mind. I don't want to get into a big fight over it. If Bea wanted to be with Chris, she'd be with him. I can't let this old woman derail our affair. *Fuck Chris and the white stallion he rode off on.*

After breakfast, I head home to do some writing. Words are flowing nicely. I have little interest in interviewing Grandma, but I remember wise advice from *The Godfather*: Keep your friends close and your enemies closer. I'll return for that interview and find the Achilles heel on that dragon.

CHAPTER SIX

Those who bring sunshine into the lives of others cannot keep it from themselves. – Sir James M. Barrie

I manage to clear a slew of emails and enjoy a late-morning workout before it's time for my interview. After cleaning up, I grab my iPad and a certain "gift" for Bea, in hopes I see her later this afternoon.

I valet at the Hyatt and go to the lobby. As I enter, a server walks past me in a huff, with smeared mascara. *What's going on here?*

Grandma didn't specify where I'd find her, so I walk through the corridor looking for a parked broomstick. The bellhop stops me.

"Mr. Silver?"

"Yes?"

"Boss is waiting for you in the lounge," he directs me.

"Thank you."

I check my watch—12:02, almost exactly on time. That should impress her. I round the divider and find Her Highness standing next to another woman who could almost be her twin. They're both reviewing a printout, and look up in eerie unison.

"You're late, blobber."

"Two minutes? Jesus. Nice to see you, too."

The woman next to Grandma is the same height, same hairstyle, and the same rimless glasses on her nose, except...

"This is my restaurant manager, Kazuko Origami."

... she's Asian. I extend a hand, which is ignored as usual.

"Why you late?"

It sounded more like 'rate' to me.

"Huh?"

"Why you late?"

"I had to wait for the valet."

"Bad excuse."

"I'm sorry, is this woman a replica of you, made in China perhaps?"

Kazuko kicks me in the shin.

"Ouch!"

"Not Chinese, fuckwad. Japanese!"

"Fine. I apologize. I was just trying to be funny."

"Not funny. Here," she hands me a polo shirt and a server's apron, "you put this on."

"Actually, I'm here to interview Ms. Aspinwald."

"You put this on."

"Ms. A? What's this about?"

"We had to let a server go, which has left us short. We have an important luncheon beginning in the Marina Room, and I told Kazuko about your gracious offer to help."

I stand there incredulously, considering my options. The Manager glares at me while holding the uniform. I can't let her win. *It's food service. I've done this. How difficult can it be? Sure, it has been thirty years, but it couldn't have changed that much.*

"All right," I agree as I take the shirt and apron. As a minor act of defiance, I put down my iPad and begin removing my T-shirt.

"What you doing? You go change in bathroom."

"I go change right here. I save time," I insist. She kicks me again. "Hey! And, no kicking or I *am* going the get all Ming Dynasty on your ass," I tease as I flex and growl like Hulk Hogan. Naturally, she kicks me again.

"Not Chinese, brobber. Japanese. You hurry. Guests waiting."

What have I gotten myself into?

CHAPTER SEVEN

Within you, I lose myself. Without you, I find myself
wanting to become lost again. – Anonymous

It turns out the luncheon is for a group of third graders. What could be worse? The little brats have their choice of pizza, grilled cheese, or chicken chunks, which is simple enough to memorize as I jot down their orders. Ms. A and Kazuko are socializing and handing out gifts, like inverted sour patch ladies—sweet on the outside, sour on the inside.

I get a quick break and step into the walk-in to cool off. I text Bea to brag about my sacrifice.

Bea Plastique: Aw, you're such a sweetie. I want to see you in your cute server outfit. I bet you look hot. ;)
Mormon Silver: Yes, aprons become me. Now if I could only find one in argyle.
Bea Plastique: Tell you what, Uncle M, let me know when you're done, and I'll give you a tour of the infamous Blue Room.
Mormon Silver: The what?
Bea Plastique: I think you'll like how it's decorated. I know I LOVE it.

As I finish reading the last text, the walk-in door opens to Kazuko.

"You slackass. Put away phone. Get movin'."

"I was ... um ... looking for the desserts."

"Ice cream in freezer, dumdum, not walk-in."

I prepare a tray of tri-flavor ice cream, and proceed out to the table. The kids are already unruly; sugar is the last thing they need. As I approach, the kids become silent and start giggling and whispering. *Who's paranoid? Me.*

Just as I fill both hands with plates, one little fucker whips out a squirt gun and start nailing me, right in the crotch. *Perfect.* I grab the gun from him.

"Very funny. Where did you get this?"

"That old lady over there gave it to me. She says you're bad, and I should squirt you in da wiener."

"Cute," I say as I glare at Grandma.

"Gimme back my gun."

"You can either have the squirt gun or the ice cream."

"But ..."

"I'll throw in five bucks. Which one will it be?"

"Ice cweam, pwease."

"Good boy."

I holster the squirt gun in my apron, give the brat a fiver, and plot my revenge. After the kids leave, the perimeter of the table looks like a war zone. Kazuko hands an odd-looking sweeping contraption to me.

"You crean."

I mumble to myself as I run over the same french fry ten times, unsuccessfully. A text pings in.

Bea Plastique: Ready, Uncle M?

Mormon Silver: Oh, you have no idea how ready, Lovergirl. Where to?

Bea Plastique: Take the elevator down to P2 underground. Look for parking space 243. Knock three times on the blue door next to it.
Mormon Silver: This better be good.

I finish sweeping kid shrapnel and another message pings in. It has an attached picture of Bea from the neck down— naked and glistening in oil—holding the camera in front of a mirror. *Slick! I'm out of here.*

CHAPTER EIGHT

A friend is one who knows us, but loves us anyway.
– Fr. Jerome Cummings

I sneak away before the two-headed beast can find me. I search for the Blue Room. When I arrive, it looks like an ordinary janitor's closet. As I reach to knock, I hear a buzz of the door unlocking. I open it and feel to the right for a light switch. It is a closet. Odd. Suddenly, the wall with shelves swings open to my glistening Lovergirl.

"Hello, Uncle M."

"This is some *Get Smart* shit right here."

"Some what?"

"Never mind. Before your time. You look delicious, my love."

"And you look ... like a server who was dragged around the beaches of Normandy," she giggles.

I'm happy, as usual, to provide entertainment.

"Ugh, no kidding."

"Ready for your tour?"

"Lead the way."

The room is a BDSM fantasy suite. There are rubberized floors, like you'd see in a gym. The walls have mirrors, TVs, and cabinets. There's blue leather furniture throughout. Bea looks sexy, shining in the subtle golden light. Nine Inch Nails' "Closer" thumps while we walk.

"What's this?" I ask as I examine a swing set with odd straps and pulleys.

"Oh, that's for advanced lovers. We need to work up to that."

"Looks like a back ache to me."

There's a laminated wooden paddle hanging on the wall next to three whips. The paddle has some obvious wear and a brass plaque with the initials CG.

"Who's CG?"

"Nobody important. Check this out," she redirects as we approach what resembles a large kid's pool with a raised rubber mattress and Velcro straps in four corners. "Wanna take a dip?"

Although distracted, the thought is not extracted. I'll find out who CG is.

"Fuck yes."

"Mm, what do you want to do me, Uncle M?"

"Well, Lovergirl, I want to strap you down, massage you nose to toes, and then fuck you in the ass so hard you'll limp for days."

"Oh my god! YES! Do it!" she commands as she dives onto the mattress and spreads her arms and legs.

I work quickly as the NIN music and the thought of conquering her luscious ass motivates me. I strap her ankles and wrists, undress myself, and climb into the oily pool. *Oil and body hair doesn't mix well. I must remember to trim.*

She arches her buttocks up toward me as I bring her to her first peak with my probing fingers. She's wet and slippery, ready for me. *Hm, this is an ideal position for interrogation.*

I kneel between her legs, reach outside the pool for my apron, and grab the squirt gun I confiscated at the luncheon. It's time for Uncle M's version of water boarding.

"What are you doing? Get inside me."

"Not quite yet. First, I want to know who CG is." *I have an idea who it might be.*

"I told you—nobody."

"Wrong answer," I respond as I squirt her in the clit.

"Hey," she squeaks.

"I'll repeat the question: Who [squirt] is [squirt] C [squirt] G?"

"Stop! Jesus. OK, fine."

"I'm waiting."

"Chris ... my ex."

That motherfucker!

"Why is his paddle here?"

"Don't you want me, Uncle M?"

I squirt her again. "Answer the question."

"He's an architect. He designed this room."

"Are you still seeing him?"

"No! I love you, Uncle M," she reassures me. Now she'll pay.

"You've been a bad Lovergirl. Now, I'm going to take my billy club to your naughty ass."

"Yes, please."

I toss the squirt gun, climb onto her, and insert myself slowly. She's so tight. The sensation gives me the urge to come in the first thrust. I reach around her right hip and stroke her clit while I slowly grind deeper and deeper. I kiss her neck, bite her ear, and lose myself in the moment, while Chris G. weighs on me.

CHAPTER NINE

The human heart feels things the eyes cannot see and things the mind cannot understand. – Anonymous

I'm tempted to leave her strapped down, but I can't bring myself to do it. As our heartbeats return to normal, Bea leads me into a side room—an amazing bathroom with black tile, a whirlpool, and a shower that rains from above. Bea turns on the shower and taps buttons on a control panel to change the mood of the music. Sade sings while we scrub the oils from each other. *I'm hard again. I can't resist her.* If this keeps up, I'll need an IV. Then again, I do love my Kindle and I'm only two orgasms away from another $25 gift card.

As we make love on the edge of the tub, my jealous thoughts of Chris G. subside. Her second orgasm is explosive as I'm beginning to learn how to push her love buttons.

We dry off, put on soft robes, and return to the play area. I fiddle with the straps on the funky swing, trying to imagine what goes where and how.

"The next time we make love, I want you to tell me exactly what you want and how you want it," I suggest.

"As long as you talk dirty to me."

"I do."

"Not really; you're more like PG. I prefer triple-X."

"Really? Like what?"

"You know."

"I don't, otherwise I'd comply ... probably. I say 'fuck' a lot. That's good, right?"

"Sure, but there *are* other naughty words."

"OK, since you're into hockey stuff, how about punishment for 'High Dicking,' 'Cross-Licking,' and 'El-blowing' penalties?"

"Funny. No, I mean other *swear* words."

"Like?"

"I can't say them. I don't swear, remember?"

"Fine. I'll say a swear word and you give me a hotness reading on a scale of one to ten, with ten being sizzling. Cool?"

"Cool."

"Pussy."

"Three."

"What? That deserves a six, minimum. All right. Cock."

"Seven."

"Hmm, better. How about twat?"

"That one depends."

"On?"

"The adjective."

"Ah, I got this. So, something like honey dripping hungry little twat is good and stinky twat is bad."

"You're catching on."

We continue playing the word games, and then Bea offers to demonstrate the swing to me.

"Let me strap you in."

"Ha! No way."

"Don't you trust me?"

"Not really."

"I'm hurt, Uncle M. Oh well. Pity. You were so close to getting that Kindle gift card."

Jesus. She knows my weaknesses.

"OK, fine. Be gentle."

"Of course."

Bea straps my wrists and ankles, and runs a harness under my lower back. The bungee straps give a bit, so I bounce playfully.

"Say, why don't you climb aboard, Lovergirl," I dare her.

"Nope."

Ah, that's right—dirty talk.

"Get your delicious cunt over here right now and straddle my fuck stick."

Her eyes widen, she drops the robe, undoes mine, and saddles up. We bounce like crazy as I wonder if the straps might give way. Orgasm number three comes in minutes as Uncle M relishes the thought of another conquest and another eBook.

Bea dismounts, walks away, and begins dressing. *Oh, no.*

"Um, Lovergirl?"

She ignores me.

"Sweetie?"

Nothing.

"Honey?"

Shit.

Bea—fully dressed now—changes the channel on the TV I'm facing. A DVD begins playing:

NHL Playoff Series, Game 1. April 24, 2008:

Montreal Canadiens 4, Philadelphia Flyers 3.

She reaches into her purse, pulls out a gift card, tosses it my way, winks, and leaves me hanging.

CHAPTER TEN

What lies behind us, and what lies before us, are tiny matters compared to what lies within us.
– Ralph Waldo Emerson

I suffer through the painful end of the overtime win by the Canadiens, wondering how to free myself. Then I hear a buzz and unlatching of the door. It swings open. *Shit. Not again.*

The same two housekeepers who caught me in a bind in Bea's suite walk in, carrying mops while giggling at my expense.

"Hello, sir. We were told there was a spill in aisle Blue."

"Har-de-fucking-har. Untie me."

"Wow, somebody's in a bad mood."

"I don't think I like his attitude," the second maid adds.

"Fine. *Please* untie me."

"That's better, but ..."

"Pretty please, with a twenty-dollar tip on top."

"As you wish."

They untie me and I try to get the circulation flowing to my hands and feet again. I gather my clothes and wallet. I peel off a twenty for my rescuers and pocket my gift card. *At least I netted five dollars and Bea's amazing posterior in the transaction. I consider myself ahead.*

I go to the valet and retrieve my Jeep. Once home, I flop onto the couch, in desperate need of a nap. Not fifteen minutes into it, my phone beeps.

37

Bea Plastique: How's it hanging, Uncle M?

Mormon Silver: I am going to beat your little butt next time I see you.

Bea Plastique: Promises, promises. Oh, and when might that be?

Mormon Silver: How about dinner at my place tonight? *I sure could use home field advantage for once.*

Bea Plastique: Sounds fun. When?

Mormon Silver: 7ish.

Bea Plastique: What can I bring?

Mormon Silver: Toppings: spray whipped cream, Hershey's syrup, and crème de menthe.

Bea Plastique: Yum!

I scurry through the grocery store gathering toy food. The checkout clerk wears an odd expression as she types the produce codes.

"Someone is planning quite the feast."

"Indeed."

"Who's the lucky girl you're going to eat this off ... I mean, with?"

I grab a banana. "Behave yourself. I'm licensed to carry, and I have a big banana."

"Ooh, even luckier."

Bea shows up fashionably late with the bag of toppings, as requested. *I'm going to devour them and her.* I make sure my *Broad Street Bullies* DVD plays while we eat dinner. Teasingly, I leave the dessert tray on the counter: bananas, strawberries, and pomegranate. I also have a fondue pot simmering with melted white chocolate.

She rushes through dinner, but I intentionally stall.

"Is it time for dessert yet?" she begs.

"Not until Uncle M has cleared his plate," I tease as I spoon another helping of green bean casserole.

She sticks out her bottom lip and crosses her arms like an infant. I laugh at her expression.

"OK, Lovergirl. Let's have dessert."

"Yay!"

She claps and grabs her bag of toppings. I gather the food tray and fondue pot, and lead her into my bedroom.

"What's this?" she asks as she sees the big blue tarp covering my bed.

"I can't afford your architect, so this baseball mound cover will have to do for my version of a Blue Room."

It's often wise to improvise.

Naturally, as we're about to dine on each other, the doorbell rings.

"Are you kidding me? If this is people here to talk about Jesus, I'm going to send them to meet him."

"I'll do a little grounds maintenance while you're gone," Bea offers as she begins undressing.

I answer the door to a deliveryman holding a dozen red roses. *WTF? Did Bea send me roses?* There's a note attached.

Dearest Bea, I hope you and your future ex-lover enjoy your break up sex. I'll be waiting. CG

Fucker!

CHAPTER ELEVEN

You come to love not by finding the perfect person,
but by seeing an imperfect person perfectly. – Sam Keen

"What is it, honey?" Bea asks from the bedroom.

"Nothing. Be right there."

I stuff the roses into the garbage disposal. It grinds loudly. Bea emerges from the bedroom, already down to her lacy undergarments. *How can I be mad at her when she's so delicious?*

"What are you doing?"

"Oh, that was a delivery for you," I inform as I hand her the card. "I was trying to water the lovely roses and, oops, they slipped into the drain."

"He's such a jerk."

"Are you absolutely certain this thing between you two is over?"

"Way over. He's a freak and I want nothing to do with him."

"Why did you break it off in the first place?"

"He's twisted. All he wanted to do was dress me, force me to eat, and spank me. I felt like cattle he was fattening for slaughter. He used to leave bruises on me."

"Sounds like *he* needs a beating."

"I know, Mormon, but he's not worth it. He's way up in Seattle anyway. Just ignore him. Please?"

"So, we're not breaking up tonight?"

"Quite the opposite, my love," she assures as she tosses the card into the garbage.

41

We scurry into the bedroom before the melted white chocolate cools.

"You first, Lovergirl," I insist as she giddily complies by removing her undergarments.

"Would you like me sunny-side up or over easy?"

"Hm. Let's start with up."

I take the cool crème de menthe and run a river from her neck to her navel. I see goose bumps. I drip a bit over my index finger and touch it teasingly to her lips. She takes my finger in and teases the tip with her tongue. *Time for another sensation.* I take a honey ladle, dip it into the thick melted chocolate, and dollop a bit on each nipple, both sides of her neck, and in the crease where her thighs meet her hips.

"Is that too hot, Lovergirl?"

"It's perfect, Uncle M."

I spray whipped cream, leaving a white stripe next to the minty green river. *This is beginning to resemble a New York Jets uniform. Not that I'm a huge football fan, but I will definitely fuck this tight end tonight.*

It's time for the fruit. While the chocolate dries on her, I take a strawberry, dip it in the fondue pot, spray a spot of cream on the tip, and feed her. We kiss while she chews. The pink juices run down her neck; I catch them and lick her clean.

We take turns coating each other and enjoying the sensations: the mix of flavors, the cool, the warm, the runny, and the firm. My Lovergirl is the most delectable treat I've ever experienced, and there will be no leftovers for CG.

A night of love wears on me as my fifty-year-old body makes me pay for my twenty-year-old thoughts. Bea dresses next to the bed as I wake up.

"Ugh. Could you dim that light please?"

"That's the sun, silly man," she giggles as she tickles my foot. "You had better get up. You have an interview in one hour."

"Huh? Oh, Jesus. Grandma?"

"Yep. She's meeting you at the E Street Cafe in Encinitas at ten."

"Shit. I have an owie," I remark while rubbing my eyes. "My head feels like someone is pinching my brain stem with needle-nose pliers."

"Here," she hands me a pill and bottle of water.

"Ibu?"

"Something like that."

I down the pill and hit the shower. Bea stops by and gives me a kiss on her way out. If I can get past her evil ancestor and abusive ex, I'm confident there's a wonderful life ahead of us.

CHAPTER TWELVE

Never let a problem to be solved become more important than the person to be loved. – Barbara Johnson

Making sure I'm not late, I zip down the coast and rumble over the train tracks. I feel an odd sensation as Little Mormon begins to rise in my jeans. *Hm, the slightest thought of my Lovergirl does this to me.*

As I park and approach the E Street Cafe, I "adjust" myself and hope the lump in my pants isn't noticeable. A text beeps in.

Bea Plastique: How's your head?
Mormon Silver: Still throbbing.
Bea Plastique: LOL! Oh, I bet.
Mormon Silver: And that's funny why?
Bea Plastique: No particular reason. Would you like Nurse Lovergirl to take a look?
Mormon Silver: Huh?
Bea Plastique: ... at the swelling? Tee, hee.
Holy shit, she can see me.
Mormon Silver: Where are you? Thought you said you had to go to the Ranch office today.
Bea Plastique: That's where I am.
Mormon Silver: Then, how can you see my swelling?

I adjust my package again. A woman sitting inside the window has noticed. She wrinkles her nose. The door opens as I send the last text; it's Grandma.

45

"Well, it's about time. Let's go. I only have an hour."

"Where's mini-she?"

"Kazuko is keeping an eye on the shop," Grandma explains as she leads me to her table. "Why are you limping? Did you hurt yourself, you clumsy oaf?"

Oh, shit. How can I spin this?

"Um, yes, I stubbed my toe on the bedpost this morning. How nice of you to care."

"I didn't say I cared, did I?"

When we arrive at her table, a tall, handsome man stands to greet me. He's wearing a gray suit and a smirk.

"Mormon, this is Chris."

Seriously? Not THE Chris!

I shake his hand and size him up. He has a good six inches, twenty years, and forty pounds of muscle on me.

"Let me guess: You're the woman-beating douche who sent me flowers."

"I sent flowers to my fiancée, Bea, actually."

"What's he doing here?" I ask Grandma.

"Look, Mormon," she toys, "we all know you're a temporary distraction for my granddaughter. She's having a tough time dealing with her fiancé being out of town so much."

"But, now that I'm back," Chris adds, "I need you to go away so we can resume our wedding plans."

"Right. Why would I do that?"

"Well, I suppose I could give you a few thousand reasons," he offers as he pulls a checkbook and pen from his vest pocket.

"Not millions?"

He presses his slimy lips into a thin line, "Mr. Silver, you should be thankful I'm offering anything as you're frankly not even worth hundreds to me."

"I see. Just so we're clear, Bea isn't worth hundreds, thousands, or millions to me—she's *priceless*. She's also a free woman who prefers to be treated like a lady, not a racehorse."

I try to stay calm, but I can feel my face flush. He definitely can beat my ass, so I'm not going there. Oddly, through all this, I now have a raging hard-on, which Grandma discovers. She shows disdain toward me as usual.

"Dear Lord, Mr. Silver. Can't you control yourself?" Grandma quips.

Great fucking timing!

I ignore her and continue. "So, Chris, put away your checkbook, stop sending flowers, and crawl back into whatever leather-walled dungeon you crawled from. You had your shot and you blew it. Bea is marrying me."

I turn to leave.

"This isn't over, Silver. She'll be mine again soon. You don't know what Bea needs; I do. She's out of your league, Silver!"

We'll see.

CHAPTER THIRTEEN

You have to walk carefully in the beginning of love; the running across fields into your lover's arms can only come later when you're sure they won't laugh if you trip.
— Jonathan Carroll

I'm fuming over his nonsense, and becoming concerned over No-Longer-Little Mormon. I'd love to work off some anger at the gym, but that's not going to happen in my current state. *Maybe a bath will do.*

I phone Bea on the way home. It goes straight to voice mail, so I call her office. Eric answers.

"How's it going, Eric?"

"Fine. And you, Mr. Silver?"

"I've seen better days. Is she around?"

"In a meeting right now. She should be done around noon. Is it an emergency?"

"Um," I hesitate, "no, not really."

"What's up?"

"Funny you should ask in such a way. I have a problem with two dicks."

"Ooh, do tell!"

"The first dick—the larger of the two—is Bea's ex, Chris. Know him?"

"I do, and you're right—he's a dick."

"He's trying to work his way back into her life by buying me off."

"An incorrigible dick."

"What you said."

"And the other dick?"

"My own, actually. For the last hour, I've had petrified wood with no signs of ever bending again."

Eric laughs.

"I'm not exaggerating ... and, I have to pee."

Eric laughs harder.

"I'm happy to amuse you."

"Oh, shit, wait. Oh my god, that crazy woman. Did you take a little yellow pill today, by chance?"

"What pill?" I ask. I can hear Eric fumble around his desk. *No way.*

"Ms. Plastique borrowed a few pills from me recently."

"What sort of pills?"

"Cialis."

Fuckity fuck bubbles. It wasn't Ibu she handed me this morning. Great.

"Well, that explains it. Now, what am I supposed to do with this?"

"It says something on the label: 'If your erection lasts more than four hours, call Eric.'"

"Very funny. And, why would Eric have such pills in his possession?"

"My *mature* boyfriend sometimes needs assistance, so we keep a supply handy."

She fucking drugged me. She will be spanked.

"Now, I have to sit around for another three hours wondering what to do with this." I pinch the swollen helmet. "Lovely."

"You could hammer down loose floorboards. Pole vault? Ring toss? Masturbate?"

50

"Right. I'm going to unload a batch, soak in the tub, and hope for the best."

"Need a hand?"

"No, Eric, I don't need a hand; I have two. Tell Bea to call me the minute she gets out of that meeting."

"Will do. Oh, and Mr. Silver?"

"Yes?"

"I'm pulling for you ... I mean with Ms. Plastique."

"Thank you, Eric."

Once home, I manage to pee through my turgidity without spraying the walls. I launch a quick batch. *Still hard.* I fill the tub and soak. My periscope points up at me, refusing to subside. *She made me this way; it's her duty to fix it.*

I dry off, dress, and drive to Bea's office. I park in the rear, climb into the back, and lie down.

Mormon Silver: I'm at your office, you naughty woman. Meet me out back when you're done with your meeting.

Bea Plastique: Why?

Mormon Silver: You know why. Two hours now. I think I'm dying.

Bea Plastique: Don't be so hard on yourself. ;)

Mormon Silver: Nice.

Bea Plastique: Wood you like to see me or not?

Mormon Silver: Oh, you're a riot, Alice.

Fifteen minutes later, I hear the clicking of her heals as she approaches my Jeep. I'm still full tilt. She peeks in the passenger window and giggles.

"Oh, my." She climbs in the passenger seat.

"You created this beast, now you're going to help me get rid of it. Get back here."

"My pleasure."

"Wait. First, open my glove compartment."

She does, and reacts like a kid opening a Christmas present as she pulls out my Fukuoku love glove.

"What's this and why is it here?"

"That *is* a glove compartment, is it not?"

"Good point."

"Bring it back here with you."

"Yes, Uncle M."

She crawls between the seats into the back and hands me the glove. She slides down her undies and opens my jeans.

"Oh, my!" she remarks at my steel beam, which is beginning to turn as purple as Prince.

I slide into the glove and turn it on low. She mounts me, reverse cowgirl style. *God, what an ass on this woman!* I reach around with my left hand and go to town on her clit as she lowers herself and grinds on my rod. *She comes quickly when Uncle M wears the glove.* I'm mostly numb, but enjoying it nonetheless. She fucks me so thoroughly that the thought of that other dick fades away ... for the time being.

CHAPTER FOURTEEN

Be able to stick with a job until it is finished. Be able to bear an injustice without having to get even. Be able to carry money without spending it. Do your duty without being supervised. – Ann Landers

After our backseat booty bouncing, I finally get a bit of bend in my bone. She flips around to face me. *Now, to other pressing matters.*

"How was your meeting with Grandma?"

"Funny you should ask. There was a special guest appearance."

"Who? Kazuko?"

"No, a big fan of yours who is becoming a festering boil on my rump."

"No!"

"Yes. Chris."

"Oh, Mormon. I'm so sorry. Did he threaten you?"

"Actually, he tried to bribe me."

"Ugh. That's how he operates. When he can't have his way he buys it."

"Yep. So, I'm five dollars richer and you're about to marry into major douchebaggery."

"That's not funny."

"He threw in a Ginsu."

"I'd like to throw a Ginsu *at* him. He has such nerve. What did he say?"

"He insists this thing between us is a tryst, and you'll return to him."

"No chance. You know this is real, my love," she insists as she touches my cheek and stares into my eyes with clarity and sincerity.

I raise my gloved hand and give her a thumbs-up. We break into laughter—two lovers, midday, in the back seat acting like horny teenagers.

"I have to get back inside. Another meeting. Why don't you meet me in the Blue Room around six tonight?"

"Hm, that might be fun." *Oh shit, stiffness is returning.*

"It most definitely will be," she assures as she leans forward, kisses my throbber, and crawls into the front.

"I almost forgot. You fucking drugged me, you maniac!"

"It was an accident."

"You will be harshly punished for this misdeed later, Lovergirl."

"I sure hope so."

Bea blows a kiss and walks back into her office. I holster my meat and climb into the driver's seat. Maybe I can get some writing done this afternoon. The distraction may persuade my blood to stop pooling in my groin.

As I pull away, my phone rings through Bluetooth; it's my buddy, Grant.

"What up, G?"

"You."

"Ha! You have no idea."

"What time should I pick you up tomorrow?"

"For?'

"The shindig. You're not driving."

"What shindig?"

"Bachelor Party, Part One at The Purple Church."

"Huh?"

"Oh, shit. Was that supposed to be a surprise?"

Who's behind this?

"Spill, dude."

"I got a Facebook event notice from Bea. Thought for sure you were on it."

"I probably am. I haven't had a chance to sign in. Been a little occupied."

What's she up to?

"So, what time? It starts at eight."

"Pick me up at seven-thirty, I guess."

"See you tomorrow."

"Cool."

A man my age shouldn't have a bachelor party; he should have a nice dinner outdoors with friends, Cuban cigars, and expensive tequila. *Fine. I'll play the role.*

CHAPTER FIFTEEN

Your words are my food, your breath my wine. You are everything to me. – Sarah Bernhard

I drive down to the Hyatt, fighting traffic all the way. I park on the level near the Blue Room and text Bea.

Mormon Silver: The package has arrived.
Bea Plastique: Ha! Is it still in its hard, protective shell?
Mormon Silver: No, luckily it has returned to its original shape.
Bea Plastique: Not lucky for me. :(Anyway, I'm running late and will be there in thirty minutes. You can go ahead in and wait for me.
Mormon Silver: I don't have a key.
Bea Plastique: Check your email. I sent you the link and code.
Mormon Silver: OK. See you soon.
Bea Plastique: And don't touch anything in there ... yet.
Mormon Silver: Yes, ma'am.

Sure enough, I have an email from her on my iPhone. I click the link and enter the code. The door buzzes open. *Fancy!* I bring along my love glove. *Time for exploration.*

I cruise around the room, inspecting the various unfamiliar instruments. Dickhead's paddle is still hanging on the wall. I have half a mind to take it to her mischievous butt. I didn't realize last time that there are additional rooms. I find one with an actual (non-rubberized) bed, a TV, and, naturally, a mirror on the ceiling. Then, I try another door, which opens to a playroom with a pool table and an air hockey machine. *Hm.*

The bed looks comfortable so I plop down on it and begin thumbing the remote. Thankfully, the video that comes into focus isn't Mormon in panties, but it *is* porn. *There's no limit to her kinkiness.* The video shows a nude brunette wearing a masquerade mask, lying on a bed next to a tray filled with assorted lubes, fruit, and vegetables. There's a dim, sexy candlelight flickering. I feel a twitch. *Looks tasty. I know I haven't had my six servings.*

The woman is playing to the camera. She drizzles lube just above her shaven pussy and allows it to drip like syrup down her luscious lips. *More twitching in my pants. Oh, boy.* She smiles toward the camera as she spreads the lube with her fingers, arching her back in pleasure. The bed and room look familiar.

She begins sampling the fruit and veggie tray, as Little Mormon begs to come out and play. First, she lubes up a healthy-sized zucchini. She inserts it a few inches, pulls it out, rubs it on her love button, and reaches to the tray for another item: a yellow squash. *Wow, she's a trooper!*

Then, I realize the bed in her video is the one I'm currently lying on. *This was filmed here? Hot!* I look beneath the TV and see a tripod stand and camera. *Thank God, the camera is off. I wonder who ... it couldn't be, could it? Shit. It is.* The woman in the video is my luscious Lovergirl wearing a wig. I should have recognized her by that amazing body.

It's hard to resist pleasuring myself while watching Lovergirl play with her food. I hear the front door buzz and welcome the voice of my vixen.

"Hello, Uncle M."

"Hello, Lovergirl."

"What are you up to?"

"Just checking out the Food Network. I never knew Rachael Ray was so talented, nor zucchini that versatile."

Bea enters the bedroom and notices my lump.

"Hard still?"

"Hard *again*. I'm dying to see what she does with eggplant. Meanwhile," I slide into my love glove, "somebody here was exceptionally fiendish today, and deserves a spanking."

"Ooh, yes, I was very bad," Bea admits as she removes her undies and dives across me, lying perpendicular across my waist. She lifts her skirt. "How many lashes shall I receive, Master?"

"Five should do. But, it will have to wait until my show is over."

She turns her head toward me and gives that pout I can't resist.

"Fine," I agree. I hit pause on the remote, turn my love glove on slow vibration, and strike her lightly on the bum.

"Was that supposed to hurt? Are you trying to punish me or tickle me?"

"I don't think I could ever bring myself to hit a woman harder than that. Sorry, sweetness. Perhaps you would accept alternative punishment in the form of a deep vaginal massage."

"Yes, please."

Once again, my glove and my love—a match made in sensuality.

CHAPTER SIXTEEN

Having sex is like playing bridge. If you don't have a good partner, you'd better have a good hand.
— Rodney Dangerfield

We frolic on the bed, which seems too ordinary for our sexual playbook; it's the running back over guard play of love. I have an idea. *She's infecting me with her kinkiness.*

"Let's have fun in the playroom," I suggest.

"I thought you'd never ask. I have to warn you, though; I'm an expert at table games."

"We'll see about that."

I peel off the glove and the two of us walk naked into the Garden of Perversion with my pet snake still under the influence.

"Wanna do it on the pool table?" she offers.

"Nope. Bad experience."

"Really?"

"Sit on my lap, and I'll tell you a story," I suggest while leading her to a barstool. "Once upon a time, the Big Bad Wolf placed Little Red Riding Slut's heels in two corner pockets and took his cue stick to her. To gain extra leverage, Wolfie dug his toesies under the lip of the pool table. This caused much discomfort and blistering of his wittle toe tops. Red also wound up with brush burned cheekie-doodles."

"You're crazy, Uncle M. That's why I love you."

"I love you back. Since you're such a hockey fan, I thought it might be fun to do it on a hockey rink that won't stick to me."

"Hmm, that is actually a virgin air hockey table."

"Not for long."

Young men don't eat enough pussy. Either that or they don't do it right. For Christ's sake, it isn't that difficult. I'm placing part of the blame on women who either lie there allowing Ole Fumble Lips to flop around missing the point, or fake it to get it over with. Find me a man who knows how to lick a woman to orgasm and I'll find you an ex-girlfriend of his who gave him specific directions and held him to a high standard of quality by demanding practice instead of unreciprocated oral treats. Ladies, please, whether your man asks for directions or not, give them to him. It's in your best interest. His next lover will appreciate it too. I only have one tongue, damn it.

I apologize for my rant. Now, back to your regularly scheduled program...

Not only do I go down on my Lovergirl like a man in a barrel over Viagra Falls, I turn the table air jets on high so she has the additional sensation of cool air blowing up her crack. Score one—actually two, for Uncle M, because I also learned how to do come hither to make her come more quickly.

Before I climb aboard and join her in O'ville, a voice blares over the intercom. It's Grandma, the wretched queen of cockblockery.

"Bea, is Mr. Silver in there with you?"

Bea goes to the phone on the wall and presses a button to respond.

"Yes, in fact he is. We're playing air hockey." She winks at me.

"Have him stop by the lounge on his way out, and by 'on his way out' I mean *now*."

"He's on his way."

I give Lovergirl my best what-the-fuck look as that bus speeds over me.

"What?" she asks innocently.

"Seriously?"

"Oh, she probably just wants to give you some money for helping out with that banquet."

"Great. I hope she gives me a bunch of ones to use at my bachelor party tomorrow night."

"Why haven't you responded to the invitation?"

"Because I can't use Facebook while having sex with you."

"Bet you can."

"I should know better than to tempt you."

We dress and part ways; Bea goes to her condo, I go to the lounge. Kazuko meets me there, throws a polo shirt at me, and hands me a church key.

"You mix drinks, Brobber."

CHAPTER SEVENTEEN

When you get back together with an old boyfriend, it's pathetic. It's like having a garage sale and buying your own stuff back. – Laura Kightlinger

Grandma's putting me to work again, trying to keep distance between lovers like a chaperone at a school dance. They never stopped me from reaching second base back in the day; she won't win this game.

"Emery not here. She sick," Kazuko explains.

Who? Oh, Emily.

"You want me to tend bar?"

"Do it. I too short."

I did some moonlighting a few years ago to catch up on my credit card bills. It was fun, actually.

"Sure, why not?"

"You go change in bathroom, or I kick monkey snot out of you," she teases. *Seems this woman is beginning to like me.*

"All right, but I'm keeping my tips."

"Twenty percent to me."

"Fifteen ... and I get to drink as much as I want."

"Go!" she directs as she smacks me on the butt.

The crowd in the lounge is mellow: conference-goers, salespeople, and tourists. I enjoy delivering therapy with martinis. People carry loads of fucked-up stories; it inspires my writing.

A lovely, young brunette bellies up and orders a lemon drop. I card her and then oblige while noticing her innocence obscured by something dark. *Pry, I must.*

"What's up, Buttercup?"

"Oh, the usual: men."

"I happen to know a few. Maybe I can help. My name is Mormon, people around these parts call me The Man Whisperer."

"Nice to meet you. I'm ...," she catches herself, "... Annie."

She extends a hand, which I shake firmly. *I hate that wet noodle shake, with either gender.*

"My boyfriend has these issues stemming from his childhood, and I'm not sure I can deal with them."

"Everyone has issues. The question is: Do you love the guy?"

"Desperately."

"Does he love you?"

"I believe he does. He proposed."

"Ah, did you accept?"

"Not yet."

"All right. What sort of issues are they?"

She takes a long drag on the lemon drop and sighs.

"He was abused as a child, so he is afraid of being touched; he gets off on spanking, restraining, and shoving metal objects into women's orifices; and he's an extremely jealous control freak."

Jesus! Another low-self-esteem woman, guilted into believing she deserves nothing better than a misogynistic beast. His fucked-upness was not her doing, and it's not her responsibility to cure his disease.

"But, he's rich and hung like a rhino," I justify, partially teasing.

"Well ..."

"Where did you meet Hungryballs Lector?"

"Up north. We're here on a mini-vacation."

Her Blackberry beeps. She bites her bottom lip.

"Don't do that, Annie."

"Don't do what?"

"Bite your lip. You'll get lipstick on your teeth and your lips will get chapped."

"Oh, sorry. Anyway, it's not like he's evil—just sexually twisted," she murmurs. *Sounds to me like she enjoys it, somewhat.*

"Look, Annie, if you think you can't find good sex with a man who will treat you like a lady, you're wrong, and you're too goddamned young to give up now."

She rolls her eyes, and takes another pull on the martini; it's gone before the sugar has settled on the rim.

"I have to go," she insists as she rises and slaps a twenty on the bar. "Keep the change, Mormon."

"Aim a little higher, Annie."

I hate to see loveliness wasted on the unworthy and unappreciative.

Kazuko checks in with me occasionally. I'm having fun with my guest bartending stint.

"You good at this. Emery razy. She tease men too much with dem big-a-boobs," she explains while gesturing as if she were holding softballs.

"Show 'em if you got 'em, is what I always say. Expose everything but the tips and you'll make more tips."

"You disgusting." She hands me a coffee mug. "Here. Put sake in it."

"Ooh, I'm telling Grandma."

"Shut up. Ode rady drive me to drink."

"Me too. Think I'll join ya," I suggest as I crack a bottle and grab another mug.

My lovely Bea arrives to check on me.

"Hey, Kazuko, how are you?"

"Fine. You boyfriend good bartender. Maybe I hire him."

"Mormon's talented in *so* many ways."

"Aw, shucks," I tease as I hand Kazuko her mug and kiss my love.

"No kissing. Work!" Kazuko orders.

"Miss Plastique, would you like a beverage?"

"Um, ok. I'll have a Shirley Temple."

"Nothing stronger?"

"No, not right now, thank you."

I mix some cherry juice and soda, considering the life ahead of me—*mixed, but not bad.*

CHAPTER EIGHTEEN

Sex at age 90 is like trying to shoot pool with a rope.
– George Burns

Bea hangs with me for a bit, and then she heads up to bed, feeling she may be coming down with something. I finish my shift, count my tips, and offer the agreed-upon commission to Kazuko on my way out. She refuses. *Cool boss!* I walk away from an interesting evening with what amounts to another ten or so books for my Kindle.

When I get to my Jeep, I realize I left my all-important Fukuoku Glove behind. *No problem; I have the code.* I find the link on my iPhone and enter the code. I can hear music blaring from the Blue Room. *Hm.*

Unsure of what I'll find, I enter the bondage arena slowly. The music is bad seventies funk—obviously a porn background track—coming from the bedroom. *She claimed she was feeling ill. Little fibber. I had better not find her being nasty without me.*

As I enter the bedroom, sure enough, there's awful big-muff porn playing on the HDTV. I notice the red light on the camera below. *Naughty girl!* When I turn toward the bed, my excitement turns to horror and my half-boner shrinks and tries to hide in my abdomen. Grandma is spread eagle with my glove on one hand and a pink Rabbit vibrator in the other.

"Silver!"

"That's my glove!" *Oh, shit. If I get a whiff of sex, I'm going to hurl.*

"Get out of here you … you … sick pervert," she yells while trying (*thank God*) to cover up.

"For the love of … my retinas are burning," I reply with a combined sensation of *ew* and *ha*.

"One word of this to anyone and you're a dead man, Silver!"

"Oh, the humanity."

I back out of the bedroom, covering my eyes, and walk out of the Gray (now) Room. Once in my Jeep, I check on my lover by calling her on my Bluetooth.

"Hey, Babydoll, how are you feeling?"

"I'm fine, just a little nauseated."

"Me, too. Do you think it was something we ate, or did I knock something loose with my massive fuck stick?"

"I'm not too sick to climb aboard Mount Mormon again."

"You should take a Tums and rest, darling."

"And, you need to get a good night's sleep because you have a big night ahead of you tomorrow."

"Ah, yes—the bachelor party. Maybe I'll bring my glove to make the lap dances more interesting. Oh, wait," I recall that evil woman, "scratch that."

"You have a free pass, my love. Take the glove. At the end of the night you're all mine."

"I'm all yours now, during, and forever after, Lovergirl."

"Good. I have something special to add to your party."

"What is it?"

"That would ruin the surprise. You'll see … and feel."

"Excellent! I hope your tummy's better. Sleep well, my love."

"You too. Love you."

"Love you back."

"Goodnight."

When I arrive at my home, there's a huge black limo parked out front. *Is this for tomorrow?* The driver's door opens. A massive man steps out and opens the back door. Fancy alligator shoes step out followed by that fuck nugget, Chris.

"What are you doing here?"

"Nice to see you too, Mr. Silver," he replies while narrowing his eyes (*is he wearing mascara?*) and offering a hand to shake.

I shake his hand. He squeezes as hard as he can. I cringe but manage to tolerate the pain as I extend my middle finger and tickle his wrist. He releases, leaps back, and wipes his hand as if it ran through a spider web.

"Quite a grip you have there, young man. Now, kindly tell me what you want, and return to your cave," I insist.

"You know what I want, Silver. Bea is mine, and this affair with you is over. Grandma has things under control at the Hyatt. Bea is coming back to Seattle with me."

"Fine," I agree as I begin unbuckling my belt. "Let's get this over with."

"What are you doing?" Chris asks while taking a step back alongside his driver.

I unzip and drop my jeans and underwear. "A duel it is. A sword fight to the death. *En garde!*" I yell while grabbing my floppy sword.

"You sick bastard," Chris answers.

I begin peeing and get some on his alligator shoes. Chris leaps backward.

71

"I smite thee! That goddamned sake; it does this to me every time."

Chris shakes his foot and holds back the driver. They have no idea how to deal with me. As they return to the limo, Chris yells, "Time is up, Silver. She's mine, you sick fuck."

"Where are you going? You're missing out on a fine vintage," I sniff. "It's an earthy nose, and, do I detect hints of green apples and asparagus? Yes, I do."

The limo drives off. I shake off and retire for the evening, wondering what Bea has in store for me tomorrow.

CHAPTER NINETEEN

*God gave man a penis and a brain, but not enough blood
to use both at the same time. – Robin Williams*

I'm finishing my domestic chores as Grant arrives to take
me to the bachelor party. Two of my friends are in the back
with road sodas.

"Damn, you guys are doing some pregame," I observe.

"You know it," a rear passenger, Joe, confirms as he hands
me a Silver Bullet.

"Too bad we don't have any entertainment for the ride,"
says Grant.

"It's all good. There will be lots of talent at The Purple
Church," I reassure him.

We arrive at the club and are escorted toward a VIP
section next to the main stage. Many of my other pals are
there, as is Kazuko. I deliver high-fives all around and give
Kazuko a big hug.

"Did you have any lap dances yet?" I ask her.

"You friends nice, but you men all pigs. I watchin' you.
Behave or I kick," she threatens.

"No worries."

I play the role, although I'd rather be taking care of my
love, who is still feeling under the weather. The ridiculous
80s big-hair music plays as the DJ announces the dancers'
silly names and reminds the men about lap dances and
special VIP dances. My boys are lining up the women for me.
I sit on my hands during the dances, reminding myself to
deliver everything to the dry cleaner on Monday.

"Next up," the DJ blares, "gentlemen, please welcome, for her very first time on stage: Lovergirl."

Fuck ... me.

Out of the back strolls my girl, wearing a silver mask and brown wig. She moves seductively to the thump of my favorite track, "Closer" by Nine Inch Nails. *Yes, I so want to fuck you like an animal, right now.*

Most of my friends haven't met Bea, and the others don't recognize her. Even Kazuko is clueless. Men begin walking up stage-side with wads of money. I'm slightly jealous, and absolutely aroused. Grant notices my excitement, walks over, gets her attention, and whispers in her ear while pointing at me. Lovergirl nods and resumes her time on the pole. *Looks like someone feels better.*

Bea collects quite a bounty as the boys make it rain. She strips all the way down to pasties and a G-string. *God, she's so fucking sexy! I'm a lucky man.*

"Gentlemen, put your hands together for Lovergirl. Great job! She'll be available for lap dances, so hit the ATM, boys."

Grant returns and plops down in the seat next to me as the server brings another bourbon rocks.

"Lovergirl is going to give you a special VIP dance. She said you should meet her in the back in five minutes."

"I'm in, Brother. That woman is delicious."

"No kidding," Grant concurs.

I take a few drags on my beverage, go toward the rear, and ask a bouncer for directions. He sends me down a corridor past a bank of rooms. Most are occupied. I approach one and do a double-take. *Holy shit!* It's Chris, and he has a woman bent over his lap—*my woman!* He spanks her hard. She squeals.

"Bea!" I yell. Chris looks up at me—his eyes wide with horror. "You piece of shit," I say as I slap him across the face. He rises up, bright red with anger. Bea gets up and turns around. *Shit. It's not Bea.* It's Annie—the woman from the bar last night. Chris is the asshole boyfriend she was telling me about.

Chris grabs me by the throat and backs me against the wall. *I'm a dead man.* I try to pry his fingers from my throat. Bea appears in the doorway.

"Chris, what are you doing? Let him go!" she insists as she grabs her stomach.

Bea vomits in front of us. It splashes on Chris' alligator shoes. Chris releases me. I gasp for air.

"Dude, I'm sorry. I thought that was Bea. Honey, are you OK? Jesus," I recoil.

Kazuko arrives to console Bea in the doorway. Bea looks up—her eyes glossed over.

"I'm pregnant."

CHAPTER TWENTY

Living at risk is jumping off the cliff and building your wings on the way down. – Ray Bradbury

That revelation presents a major problem for me as Chris, Annie, Kazuko, and I all say in unison, "What?"

"I'm pregnant," Bea repeats.

"That's nice Bea, but I'm sterile. I had a vasectomy last March," I respond, trying to suppress my anger and confusion.

"I know."

"You *know*?"

"Yes. The four fluids; remember?"

I turn my attention to Chris, as does Annie.

"Don't look at me," Chris professes while raising his hands.

"It's not yours either, asshole," Bea assures him.

Whoa, she swore!

"Thank God," Chris responds, while wiping his brow.

"Wait a minute, then whose is it?" I ask.

Jesus. There's yet another ex I need to deal with?

"I don't know."

"What do you mean, you don't know?"

"I used a sperm donor. Mormon, this was before we met. I didn't want to bring it up and scare you away."

"Yeah, well, guess what? I'm not scared. Oh," I turn toward Chris, "and she's right, you *are* an asshole."

Chris raises his big mitt to my throat again. Instantly, Kazuko springs to action, stands between us, and pushes Chris back. She's so tiny; she barely comes up to his chest.

"Touch him again and prepare to die," Kazuko threatens. Chris has no idea what to make of her as he lets go of my throat.

"Fuck you, old woman. I'll beat your ass too."

"Try it," Kazuko dares as she digs into her pocket.

What will it be? Nunchucks? A Throwing Star?

Kazuko pulls out a Marlboro and a lighter as we all watch, trying to understand what this crazy woman is up to. She lights the tip and takes a long drag—making the tip glow bright orange. She blows the smoke in his face and changes her grip on the cigarette, holding it like a knife. Chris goes pale gray, then white. He screams a guttural cry, turns, and runs out like frightened cat. Annie shrugs and follows him.

"What the ..."

"You don't want to know," Bea insists.

Pussy.

I step over Bea's mess and console her.

"Baby, are you OK?"

"Just queasy. You're not mad?"

"Why would I be mad? I love you, Bea—every inch, every toy, every passenger. If you are considering me for the role of parent to your child, I'm honored."

"Of course! It would be *our* child. I love so you much, Daddy Mormon," she cries as she hugs and tries to kiss me.

"Um, yeah, I love you back. Now," I respond as I pull away a bit, "let's get you some Listerine, and then we'll have that kiss. Cool?"

"Cool."

Love draws us along a twisted path, with unexpected obstacles, leading to beautiful new pastures. There's no one I'd rather share this trip with than my Lovergirl.

THE MIDDLE.

ABOUT THE AUTHOR

Please join the fun by following my rants at PhilTorcivia.blogspot.com, Facebook.com/SuchaNiceGuy, and Twitter.com/PhilTorcivia.

My other books, available in paperback and e-book formats:

- *Such a Nice Guy* (October 2009)
- *Still a Nice Guy* (April 2010)
- *Nice Meeting You* (October 2010)
- *Just a Nice Guy* (April 2011)
- *What a Nice Guy* (September 2011)
- *Nice Knowing You* (February 2012)
- *The 10/60 Diet: How to lose 10% of your body weight in 60 days.* (May 2011)
- *Fifty Shades of Silver Hair and Socks* (May 2012)

17250278R00043

Made in the USA
Lexington, KY
05 September 2012